Contents

The white whales

Beluga whales are easy to spot in the ocean. They have white skin and a big round forehead called a melon. Like all whales, belugas are mammals.

Belugas are small whales.
They are about 4.6 metres
(15 feet) long. Belugas
can weigh as much as
1,360 kilograms (3,000 pounds).

Up close

Belugas can hear and see well in water. To swim, they move their flukes. They can swim forwards and backwards. Pectoral fins help them to steer.

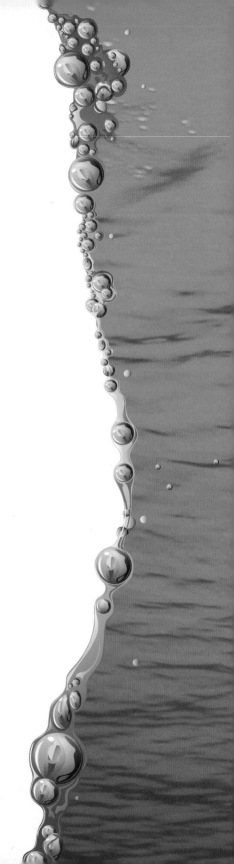

flukes

pectoral fins

Belugas swim in shallow water. But they dive as deep as 647 metres (2,123 feet)! Belugas come to the surface to breathe. Their blowholes open to take in air.

Where do belugas live?

Beluga whales live in the Arctic Ocean. The water there is very cold. Thick layers of blubber keep belugas warm.

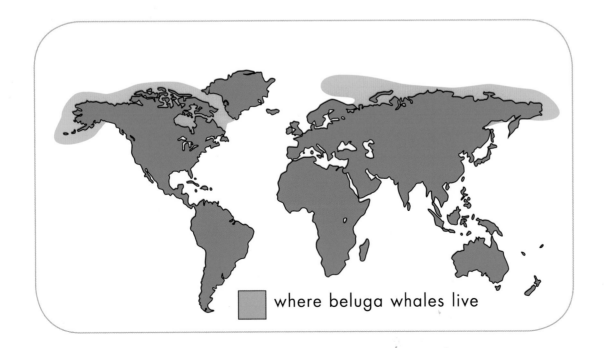

where beluga whales live

When the Arctic Ocean freezes,
beluga whales migrate south.
They live and travel in pods.
A pod can have a few whales
or hundreds.

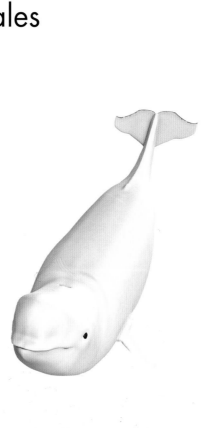

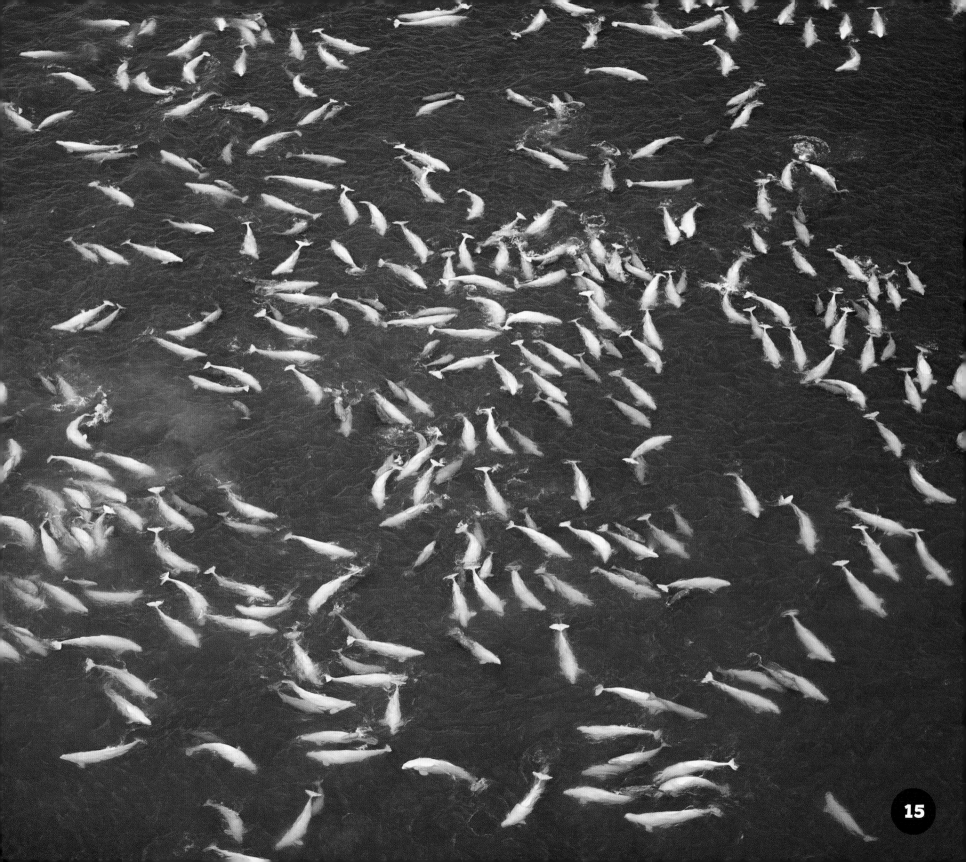

15

Life as a beluga

Beluga whales use sounds and echoes to find prey. This process is called echolocation. Belugas eat octopuses, squid, crabs, snails and fish.

Belugas love to make noise!
They communicate using clicks,
whistles and clangs. They can
even copy human sounds.

Baby beluga whales are called calves. They are born grey or brown. Calves turn white when they are 6 or 7 years old. Beluga whales live for 30 to 35 years.

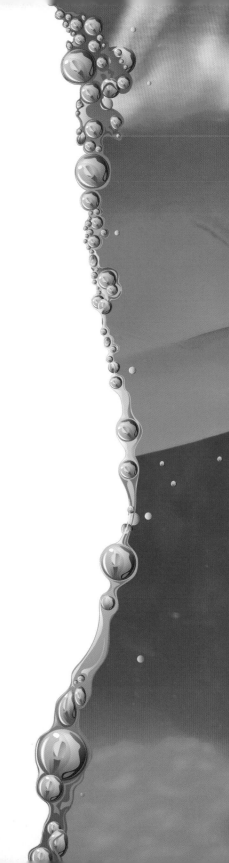

Glossary

blowhole hole on the top of a whale's head; whales breathe air through blowholes

blubber thick layer of fat under the skin of some animals; blubber keeps animals warm

echolocation use of sounds and echoes to locate objects; whales and dolphins use echolocation to find food

fluke wide, flat area at the end of a whale's tail; whales move their flukes to swim

mammal warm–blooded animal that breathes air; mammals have hair or fur; female mammals feed milk to their young

migrate move from one place to another

pectoral fins pair of fins found on each side of the head

pod group of whales; beluga whale pods range from fewer than five whales to several hundred whales

prey animal hunted by another animal for food

shallow not deep

surface outside or outermost layer of something

Read more

Animals that Hunt (Adapted to Survive), Angela Royston (Raintree, 2014)

Killer Whales (Predator Profiles), Christine Zuchora-Walske (Raintree, 2015)

Orcas (Animal Abilities), Anna Claybourne (Raintree, 2014)

Websites

www.bbc.co.uk/nature/life/Monodontidae
Learn more about white whales.

www.bbc.co.uk/nature/life/Cetacea
Discover more about whales, dolphins and porpoises.

Index